A View from the Litter Box

A Guide to Life from Miss Behavin'

Written by Gail Gastfield and Richard Record
Illustrated by Gail Gastfield

Published by Walrus Productions

Published by Walrus Productions,
4805 NE 106th St., Seattle, WA 98125, (206) 364-4365

Written by Gail Gastfield and Richard Record. Illustrations, layout and typography by Gail Gastfield.

Printed by Vaughan Printing, Nashville, Tennessee

Library of Congress Catalog Number 97-061369

Gastfield, Gail.
  A View from the Litter Box / by Gail Gastfield & Richard Record; illustrated by Gail Gastfield -- 1st ed.
  p. cm.
  ISBN 0-9635176-5-1
  1. Cats -- Humor. 2. Cats -- Humor--Pictorial works. I. Record, Richard. II. Title.

PN6231.C23G37 1997   817'.5408036
                                            QBI97-40811

Printed in the United States of America
10 9 8 7 6 5 4 3 2

Introducing Miss Behavin'

My name is Miss Behavin'. I'm a cat.
Embodiment of virtue and all grace.
I am the household's true aristocrat.
Its queen. The four pawed ruler of this place.

Though modesty incarnate, I surmise,
As one of noble bearing and outlook,
That obligation burdens one so wise.
My duty clear, I *had* to write a book.

In *A View from the Litter Box* I share
My sage advice to tickle and inspire
For literate grimalkins everywhere
And those two legged companions we require.

Therefore, with gracious charm I have unfurled
My observations on the feline world.

The Cat's Proper Place in the World

Miss Behavin': She Who Must Be Obeyed

Remember who's really in charge here.

It never hurts to ask for what you want.

Being a cat is better than being royalty; your subjects are more faithful and you don't have to worry about the tabloids.

Power may corrupt, but absolute power is delightful.

6

Leisure: it's not a life style, it's a calling.

Be the consummate individualist with definite ideas about the people you own.

Cats do nothing much in particular but they do it very well.

Be innovative in the methods used to draw attention to yourself.

Leashes – they separate the cats from the dogs.

The whole world is yours.
Observe it from high perches.

The books on the shelf read (left to right):
A Tale of Two Kitties
Puss in Boots
The Three MusCaters
The Cat of Monte Cristo
Catasppurd

9

Hop up on that pedestal
where you belong.

Just laze around while you
permit the world to reshape
itself to suit you.

Put down a firm paw every
once in a while.

Demand your rightful place,
the center of attention.

Assume that everyone is here to serve you. If they appear reluctant, keep trying to convince them.

Give in to others' wishes only when it suits your purpose as well.

Establish your territory: pick your favorite eating and sleeping spots.

When riding in a car, the best place to sit is in the driver's lap.

Part of the advantage of being a cat: no matter how naughty you are, you're never in the doghouse.

The Feline Agenda

Remember your chief duty as the guardian of the family agenda; anything you want to do is acceptable at any time.

The first thing you need to do every morning is wake up your human servant.

Standing on the chest and yowling in the face will usually arouse attention.

Batting objects off furniture may also work.

Hair-chewing, face-licking, toe-biting or face-walking are effective options as well.

Force everyone else to adapt to your schedule: when you want to play or eat, wake them up.

5am Wake them up
6 Eat
7 Nap
8 sleep
9 Scratch furniture
10 Nap
11 sleep
12 eat

1pm nap
2 Sleep in Sun
3 Play in Garden
4 Nap
5 sleep
6 Eat
7 Nap
8 Prowl the house

14

Get underfoot when everyone else is rushing around.

Trash the house when they go on vacation.

Disappear whenever the cat carrier is brought out. If it's too late to hide, puff yourself up until you're too big to fit into the carrier.

Make them work around you.

Take time to admire the view
from every window.

Greet each new day with a yowl.

Zip around in the middle of the night.

Vanish every now and then.

Come and go as you please.

Never be satisfied whether you're outside or inside; you're always on the wrong side of the door.

Wherever you go, there you are.

Your Intellectual Side

Only learn the important human words, like "food", "dinner", "sleep", "play", "meat", "nap", etc.

"No" means "try again".

Some humans talk baby talk to cats. This is one reason you have claws.

Cats are natural intellectuals because we eat a lot of fish.

Learn to appreciate good books; they make the perfect resting surface whenever someone else is trying to read them.

26 Effective Habits of Successful Cats – Essential ABC's for Life

Act as if the world is yours.

Be a nuisance at the most inconvenient times.

Claw your way to the top.

Develop strategies for blaming others.

Exist for no one's happiness but your own.

Flick your tail in their faces.

Grab hold with your claws and never let go.

Hiss at strangers.

Intimidate others with your stare.

Jump on them when they least expect it.

Kick up a little litter every day.

Let your tail do your talking.

Make them think you're listening.

Nap as much as possible.

Oversleep, overindulge, overwhelm and overcome.

Practice random acts of mischief.

Quash your enemies.

Refuse any attempts at training.

Seek out new adventures in ordinary places.

Tread silently and carry a big fur ball.

Use silence to your best advantage.

Value yourself above everything.

Wake up in time for meals.

e**X**ercise as little as possible.

Yowl until you get what you want.

Zero in on your target and pounce.

Food –
Comestibles & Digestibles

Mealtime is basically whenever you're hungry.

Some think that eating is a matter of life or death but it's much more serious than that.

Partake daily of the 4 major food groups: fish, fowl, rodents and reptiles.

Be alert to the sounds associated with food: the can opener, refrigerator and cupboard doors opening, footsteps in the kitchen, water running...

Food tastes better when it belongs to someone else.

It's impossible to sleep
on an empty stomach.

So many mice, so few recipes.

Hell has no fury like a cat unfed.

Surrender to hunger as the guiding force in your life.

When it comes to food, more is better.

If you don't know what it is, don't eat it.

Your mood usually improves with food.

Nothing succeeds like excess.

There's always enough to go around as long as you get it first.

Less is more (more or less unacceptable, that is).

If a little bird comes to tell you a secret, have him for lunch.

You may be overfed, but you're worth it.

Any food left out is fair game.

If you can't get what you want at home, try the people next door.

If it's not perfect, send it back.

Persnicketiness commands respect.

Just after your human buys a case of your favorite food, demand a new flavor.

It's important to play with your food.

Bring your live rat into the kitchen or living room where there are lots of places to corner the rascal. Be sure to leave a few remains for the humans as a tip for providing the accommodations.

Try not to fall in when taking a drink.

Anything that moves might make a good meal.

Birds of a feather taste good together.

Never trust a skinny cat.

Eating is life, the rest is just details.

Finickiness is not a character flaw.

When in doubt, sniff and nibble.

A bowl of milk, a lot of fish and ME!

Wake up and smell the caviar.

Life is too short to eat cheap food.

39

When someone criticizes your weight,
try to keep a stiff upper chin.

Remember you are not fat,
you are Rubenesque.

Emotional Development
(Caution: Potentially Explosive Moods)

Nurture your wild mood swings.

Do *not* be easily amused.

Express yourself.

Demand to be pampered.

Purring is a safety valve for contentment overload.

When bored, flash a cattitude.

Create your own reality.

Look adorable when
you misbehave.

Try to maintain a balanced lifestyle.

48

When under stress, count to ten and purr.

You can be trusted as long as the food is beyond your reach.

Get in touch with your inner kitten.

Harbor no remorse.

Quiver at nothing.

Don't worry, be nappy.

To thine own selfishness be true.

Feeling a little cranky? Take a catnip break.

Purr for your own pleasure only.

Have the courage to live by your impulses.

Mew softly but keep your claws sharp.

Never let them know exactly what you're feeling.

Teach others how to meditate.

Use your ears and tail to telegraph your moods.

51

The Fastidious Feline
(Health, Hygiene and Grooming)

To a cat, cleanliness is *above* godliness.

Cats are efficient self-cleaning units, with just a lick or two you always look good.

Always wash up after meals.

To wash your face, lick your paws and then rub them over your head. (Other areas of the body are readily available to the tongue).

Sharpen your claws on a waterbed.

No matter what, try to look elegant.

Don't do cute.

Never allow anyone
to dress you up.

54

Never scratch your own ears when you can get someone else to do it for you.

Use accidents as revenge; when you're being ignored, pee in their shoes.

When they go on vacation, leave little mementoes around for their homecoming.

Spread your fur freely on clothing and furniture, especially on those pieces which contrast with your coat.

Soak up the sun,
whenever you find it.

Establish several "sun thrones"
throughout the house.

Avoid chewing on electrical cords.

58

Never allow anyone to rub you the wrong way or in the wrong places (only you know what they are).

Hide your messes and blame someone else.

Vanity of vanities! All is vanity... So, what's your point?

Kicking a little litter around is expected.

The best time and place to hack a fur ball is in front of company.

A weekly roll in the dirt is good for your coat.

61

The litter box is always cleaner on the other side.

If they try to teach you to use their toilet as a litter box, just stare at them patiently until they give up.

Miss Behavin'

63

For mild tummy troubles, eat a little grass.

A nap in the sun will cure almost anything.

A sleek, luxurious coat is just one of the purrks of being a cat.

Shed at will. White fur on black clothes makes a genuine fashion statement.

Try to maintain good posture by occasionally walking around with your nose in the air.

If you associate with dogs, you'll end up with fleas.

Exercise and Fitness – Developing Claws of Steel

You don't need to join expensive fitness clubs; the whole house is your gym.

Do your warm up stretches by scratching the newest piece of furniture.

Climbing drapery is a good upper-body workout.

If you're a little overweight, try to arrange yourself in slimming poses.

Remember, even a fat cat can walk thin.

Dart around after nothing at all.

If you get a little exercise, you can eat more.

Staring contests are effective low-impact workouts.

When in doubt, chase something.

Any goal is reachable if you just grab hold with your claws.

Caution: some window coverings were not meant for climbing.

Practice aerobatics by diving off bookshelves or the refrigerator.

Randomly zoom around everyone's legs for race training.

Make the rounds of the house daily to check out your food dishes, windows, chairs and favorite hiding places.

Jumping onto and off high places strengthens important muscles.

Set your sights high on your way to the top.

When you climb a tree, be sure
you know how to get down.

Strengthen your tail by knocking around various objects; start with keys and work up to lamps.

When you get the urge to exercise, sometimes it's best to just wait until the feeling goes away.

A hearty yawn and stretch are effective exercises.

When you hear people debating whether cats always land on their feet, run!

Beware of freshly waxed floors.

If you fall on your way to the top,
try to land on your feet.

Social Skills –
Purrfecting your Purrsonality

Disturb the neighbors.

Make them wonder
what you've been up to.

Act loving only to get
what you want.

Ignore anyone who
calls you.

78

Vary your reactions to people: ignore them one minute and annoy them the next.

Make yourself the center of attention.

Cats never need assertiveness training.

Refuse to get along with kittens or puppies.

When in trouble, blame it on somebody else.

Keep your love for yourself.

Nose around wherever you like.

Mesmerize them with your eyes.

Win all the staring competitions.

Stare down your enemies.

Remember, it's not easy being charming, dignified and amusing, but someone has to do it.

83

Don't take "no" for an answer.

When meeting a stranger, try to put your best paw forward.

Always maintain your dignity and reserve.

Confuse everyone by periodically refusing to sit in your favorite spot.

Pester people when they're on the phone.

Don't get angry, get revenge.

When you're being ignored, knock over a few knickknacks.

Sniff out the allergic or phobic person in the room and snuggle up.

A nudge or two with the nose will often get you what you want.

Establish the proper pecking order with other pets by the occasional hiss and threatening stare.

Do *not* be easily amused.

85

When you're scolded, sulk for days.

87

Arch your back and hiss at nothing.

When you get caught with your paw in the cookie jar, pretend it was an accident.

Don't waste time trying to fight fair.

Hiss in the face of danger, then run and hide.

If it appears that there might be trouble, be sure you're the one to start it.

Cultivate a piercing meow.

Disdain them. Dismiss them. Distress them.

Sleeping and Naps

The enterprise of sleeping holds a great deal of fascination for cats.

Any soft warm spot can be a bed. Warm laundry, bath towels, grocery bags, wool sweaters are all acceptable napping spots.

Choice sleeping areas include: bookshelves, heat vents, dresser drawers, cupboards, closet shelves, any piece of furniture, the middle of the hall, etc.

Avoid any bed specifically intended for your use.

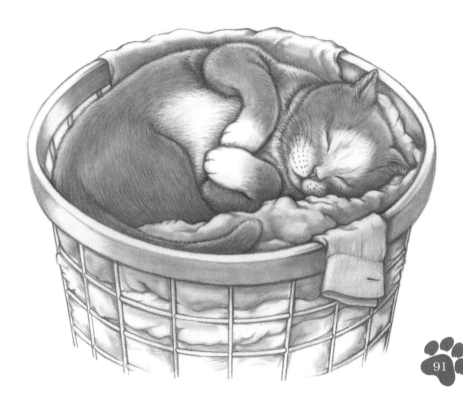

91

Demonstrate your talent for sleeping in any position, wherever and whenever you want.

Develop all your nap styles: the curl, the stretch, the roll, the flop and the blob.

93

Don't allow them to make the bed; warm, crumpled bed covers make a purrfect nest for catnapping.

Stay on guard, even when asleep.

Sleep is a journey *and* a destination.

When it comes to sleeping, practice makes purrfect.

Teach the rest of the world how to relax properly.

Nothing makes sense before noon (except food).

Get plenty of beauty rest (at least 18 hours a day).

Take frequent, regular catnaps to regain your strength.

There is no such thing as an insomniac cat.

When life gets you down, just take a nap.

It's best to let sleeping cats lie.

Don't sleep alone when you can snooze on someone's chest, lap or face.

Sleep may be habit-forming, but it is perfectly safe and easy to use.

It's great to do nothing and then rest afterward.

Nap *on* the dryer, not in the dryer.

There's no such thing as too much sleep.

Arts, Crafts & Needlework –
your pattern for self expression

Decorate the hood of the car with muddy paw prints; that's why it's there.

Develop shedding as a fine art, leaving your hair where it will attract the most notice.

Practice your interior decorating skills by rearranging the knickknacks.

Put your paw prints in fresh concrete.

Be creative: track wet paint throughout the house.

101

People can always use a little help with their knitting.

Gardening – your opportunity to get down and dirty

The garden is your jungle for prowling.

A little nibbling on the plants keeps them healthy.

Sleep in the garden on hot summer days.

Plant some catnip.

Avoid cacti.

Chase some butterflies.

Take time to eat the roses.

A garden is just one big litter box with a good view.

Computing –
just another cat and mouse game

Surf the web but don't get trapped in the net.

Join in *le chat* rooms on the Internet.

It's not called a mouse for nothing. Go for it!

Select and delete only the most important files.

Be careful not to overdo the keyboarding to avoid carpal tunnel paw syndrome.

Don't bother reading the manuals, just chew them.

The computer's mouse: great toy, bad snack.

When you're being ignored, walk or sit on the keyboard.

Hunting & Fishing – Hail to the Cat, the Predator-in-Chief

Some of the best fishing holes
are right at home.

Some days it's fish or eat bait.

Carefully position yourself to ambush your prey.

Don't keep your kill to yourself; people always appreciate a dead rodent or two.

When the red, red robin comes bob, bob, bobbin' along... deck him!

It's okay to play with your prey.

Follow your natural instincts, hunt at night.

Behold the birds of the air... but the canary in the cage is closer.

Try to look bigger when approaching your enemies.

It's easy to be brave from a safe distance.

A bird in the paw is worth two in the bush.

After a victory, sharpen your claws.

Staking out the bird feeder is always
a good hunting strategy.

113

Toys and Playing –
You can never have too much fun

Bags and boxes make dandy toys.

Investigate all containers for toy potential, but avoid getting your head stuck in a jar.

Don't play with cat toys when a paper bag or waste basket is available.

Everything in the house has toy potential.

Rubber bands are fun playthings, but refrain from eating them.

Make the office your playground: computer mice, pens, pencils were all made to entertain you.

The best toys in life are free.

Any man's trash is this
cat's treasure.

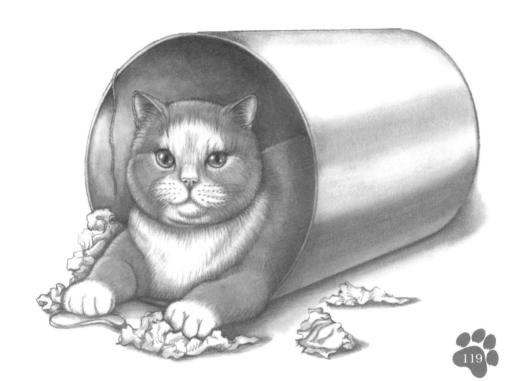

Don't be satisfied with the standard pet toys; toilet paper is much more fun.

121

Real cats don't play ball.

122

It is especially enjoyable to play with pens and pencils while humans are trying to use them.

Learn how to open doors and drawers; there are lots more toys inside.

Deign to play with your human servants now and then; when you get bored, just walk away.

Expensive antique lamps are great noisemakers.

Learn how to use the remote control and other electronic toys.

Holidays and
Other Special Occasions

(This is as jolly as I get.)

The closer to Christmas, the nicer you should act.

Of course you could just be naughty and save Santa the trip.

Don't wait until Christmas to open your gifts.

Christmas is a joy; they bring a tree indoors for you to climb and hang ornaments for you to bat.

Shred the wrapping paper on the gifts under the tree.

Don't eat tinsel, lights or ornaments.

Put coal in everyone else's stockings.

 Remember, Christmas isn't over until the fat cat eats all the cookies.

127

128

Be a loving Valentine only to get what you want.

Thanksgiving is one of the best holidays; there are always plenty of leftovers.

During family holiday meals, position yourself under the children since they tend to drop more food your way.

On Thanksgiving, don't try to eat more than you can lift.

Your best strategy on July 4th and New Year's Eve is to hide as soon as the fireworks come out.

Your birthday is another opportunity for you to be spoiled rotten.

Who says you can't have your cake and eat it too? But don't eat the candles.

Getting older's not that bad; just think of all the extra naps.

Things could be worse; consider how old you'd be in dog years.

You can usually get away with anything on your birthday.

Forget the celebration,
just go for the presents.

133

Cats are the Best because...

You never have to take a cat to an expensive salon for grooming.

The floors of a cat's home can survive without newspaper protection.

Cats are more entertaining and last longer than hamsters and goldfish.

Since cats are paragons of stress management, they never require psychiatric help.

Cats are the only soft, fuzzy lap warmers that purr.

Cats are low maintenance and self cleaning.

A cat wouldn't think of eating rotten garbage or rolling in even nastier stuff.

Cats don't howl along with your music; we prefer solo performances.

You don't have to walk a cat.

Cats don't sit under the table and beg; we just hop up and help ourselves.

A cat won't lift his leg on your leg.

Cats never chase cars.

The windows of a cat's home are free from drool and snotty nose prints.

Cats entertain themselves and don't require a lot of expensive toys or other companions.

An amorous cat knows the difference between a person's leg and another cat.

A cat won't pee on you when you rub her tummy.

Cats don't leave bones around all over the yard.

A cute little kitten will not become a 100 lb. lap cat.

With cats, you never have to contend with slimy, slobber-soaked tennis balls.

You don't have to follow a cat around with a pooper-scooper or plastic bags.

You never see "Beware of Cat" signs.

Obedience School is a laughable waste of time and money for a cat.

When the party is interrupted by a gaseous stench, no one accuses the cat.

Miss Behavin' Tries her Paw at Poetry

Haiku for Cats

unrelenting stare
cats supremely confident
humans must blink first

        tantalizing joy
        leftover tuna morsels
        clinging to my whiskers

                sunlit gossamer
                morning flight of butterflies
                cat's paws swing in play

Kitty Limericks

I tell you the truth. It's no fable.
When people put food on the table,
    By day or by night
    It is simply my right
To devour anything I am able.

      There once was an overgrown kitten
      Who crawled in a basket of knittin'
         Then proceeded to spread
         All the yarn on her head.
      This kitten was smitten with knittin'.

143

Ode on a Dinner Offering by Dr. Mews

Dry cat food? Nonsense! Are you crazed?
For dinner? Never! I'm amazed.
You contemplate such silliness?
It's met with utmost chilliness!
This meal is only fit for dogs!
They have no palates! They'd eat logs!
But I'm not Rover! I'm not Rags!
I will not eat dry food from bags!

I'll gladly dine on rigatoni,
Lobster bisque or abalone.
But here I must reiterate
And leave no room to speculate,
In spite of pleas or crying jags,
I will not eat dry food from bags!

144

With food I'm tolerance itself.
I'll take whatever's on the shelf
So long as I can pick and choose
Which things to eat, which to refuse.

It is my right! It is my due!
Demanding: moi! Complying: you!
So stop your pouting. Dry that tear.
My final meow on this is clear.
No matter who entreats or nags,
Not though the Dow Jones average sags,
Or nations all run up white flags,
I will not eat dry food from bags!

At least, that is the way I feel today.
Tomorrow, I'll have something else to say.

Metaphysical Reflections – Embracing the Mew Age

147

And God said to Adam, "Thou shalt have dominion over every living creature that moves upon the earth... that is, of course, except for the cats."

Blessed are the meek, for they shall be my dinner.

Do not let the sun go down on your anger... stay up and fight.

I yowl therefore I am.

To mew or not to mew, that is the question.

No bird soars too high
if you catch him first.

When life coughs up fur balls, knit mittens.

The self-made cat rightfully worships its creator.

Life is what happens while you're sleeping.

If at first you don't succeed, move along to something else.

What goes around, comes around... like fleas.

A cat's reach must exceed its grasp or what's a curtain for?

The question is not whether your dish is half empty or half full; the question is when will it be filled.

Take time to sit and stare.

When you have to choose between two evils, pick the one you haven't tried before.

If you live life in the fast lane, you'll get to the other end too soon.

A fool and his catnip are soon parted.

When you find yourself in a fine kettle of fish, celebrate!

During any life a little fur must fly.

Why visualize world peace when mischief and mayhem are much more fun?

Leave paw prints on their hearts and claw marks on their furniture.

The End

About the Authors

Miss Behavin' purred her advice to Gail Gastfield and Richard Record. Gail worked many years as art director and in-house artist for a poster publisher, developing designs for hundreds of posters and other products, ranging from dragons to teddy bears. She created another feline character, Roosevelt, whose grumpy face appears on T-shirts and coffee mugs. Now a freelance artist, Gail creates artwork for reproduction on apparel, posters and other gift products.

Richard works as an Internet webmaster but has always dabbled in writing. He has written several plays and co-authored a musical comedy. Richard and Gail have been married for nearly 20 years and live in Mukilteo, Washington with a few hundred teddy bears.

OTHER FUN BOOKS

A whimsical collection of delightful books to
make you think, chuckle, self-motivate & lift your spirits.

The Road to Success

Motherhood

Achieve Your Dreams

Computer Byte?

Kitty Litterature

Doggie Tales